Poetry about Life Love & Other Sh*t

Written & Designed by: Tamika Nicole
Illustrations by: Alexis Beaton

ISBN – 978-0-578-77223-3

Interior formatting by Gabriella Messina/GM Book Goods

CONTACT INFO
3HIRD EYE VIEW PUBLISHING
P.O. BOX 193
HADDONFIELD NJ 08033
feedback@tamikaryant.com

Contents

Acknowledgements

I've been through too much not to worship HIM… so first and foremost and as always I thank GOD for the gifts and visions that he has embedded in me. It was up to me to execute them, faith without work is dead.

Thank you to my daughters Anyae & Amirah, my god-daughter Tanae, my sistas Tynisha, Aikia, Valissa and Shay. My cousins Erica and Dionne, my close friends; Jane, Rashad, Theresa, Bev, Sherrick, Eric, Tez, Ratah and Keenan, for all the times I have said "Tell me what you think…You like it?" I know I worked everyone's last nerve on this project but more importantly thank you for giving me your honest opinions during the process.

To EA thank you for always using your platform in radio to promote me and all of my endeavors.

My Illustrator Alexis Beaton for giving me exactly what I asked for.

My personal assistant Jamillah Robinson for holding me down.

I appreciate all of you!!... Now let's get into this book!

Test = Testimony

Pain = Purpose

Favor Blessing Covered

But GOD

Never did mind taking the road less traveled

but through my travels

I refused to be defeated in this rat race

someone please come help pull me out this crawl space

I need more room

to breathe

I need more room

to be free

God told me he had a plan

gave me visions that I didn't fully understand

See this whole time I didn't realize He was testing me

turning my pain into my purpose to bring out the best in me

So this box that they put me in will not be my nemesis nor will it be my

destiny

I will not die full but I will die empty.

I Like You... (Part 1)

Something intriguing that caught my attention the first time I laid eyes
on you
can't quite put my finger on it
but it was like I could read you after only speaking a few words to you
It's just something so familiar, and my words can't get no realer -then
this -
Mmm... and then we kissed
Your voice, your smile, your teeth, your lips
and I have to admit you won me over with your smile, then other
things after a while
And please this is far from a come on line
but this shit got me wondering if perhaps we ever met in another
lifetime
So ....have we met before?
cause if not, it gives me something to look forward to
like the endless possibilities of things that you and I could do
and it makes me kinda glad that we never crossed paths in the past-
cause-
we might not be sitting here today

I'm just saying

it could have been a few factors like

people, places, and things that could have got in the way

Would you like to know my impressions of you so far………. let's see

well-seasoned, straight shooter, fast talker, lil cocky wild child with a

deceiving smile

and just know, I just need you to be you

You don't have to impress me

just don't lie to me, bring no drama to me and please don't disrespect

me

and if you can leave that street shit in the streets shiiid

then we might be on one

Fuck around and be on to something

you and I could have a long run

So now that you have my attention, let's see if you can keep it

last nigga put up a high score, let's see if you can beat it

and now that you got a taste of these oils let's see if you gone leak it

I guess what I'm tryna say…..

wait hold tight I'm just a line away

Is that I like you……. I really really like you

and if you last long enough, maybe I'll have enough substance for a

part two

But before I go, just a few words of advice

I'm good to those that are good to me, so make sure you treat me right

and I promise you're going to love me and you'll have a friend in me

for life

Pandemic

*

Epidemic turned pandemic
they told us we had nothing to worry about
and we ran with it
weeks later thousands of people were infected with it

Every day you hear the words unprecedented times and uncharted
waters
in an economy where families are already struggling to feed their sons
and daughters
deaths are at an alarming rate
our population is starting to dissipate

and no tax bracket or class can separate
no one is safe

No one is exempt

Hard to tell if the government really cares about people getting sick
or is it just- politics
as usual
we watched the usual become the unusual
where the new norm is shopping with gloves and mask on

And I'm still a little weary – not sure if I'm buying into the conspiracy
theories

Are they counting us and killing us at the same time

Are we over populated?

Are they that calculated?

Do you hear HIM? ……..God is calling
we all better get on our knees and pray before the sky start falling

Instead of gearing up for survival mode, we should be gearing up for
revival mode
because bottom line is -*God is still in control* –
Hugs and daps to the essential front line workers carrying a lot of
weight on their backs
thank you for your selfless acts
and services
I just hope we all keep that same energy and continue to love one
another when all of this is over

Worse than the Great Depression
time we start asking ourselves some trivial questions
and I hope we all took this time to do some self-reflecting
mail in ballots for election
so they can fuck us on the back end

Even with a vaccine it's not over yet
see this intangible thing has a domino effect
closed businesses means lost wages and households with no paychecks
our economy unsustainable
and for some daily living is no longer maintainable

I have a heavy heart

Mental health issues and depression
now back to my question
GOD is calling……………Do hear HIM now?
and that's a loaded question

This is one for the books, never thought I'd be living through some
shit I read about in my history books

COVID-19 is one of the surrealist things I've ever seen

So please don't ask to come over or ask me out during this quarantine

GOD is calling – Do you hear HIM now?

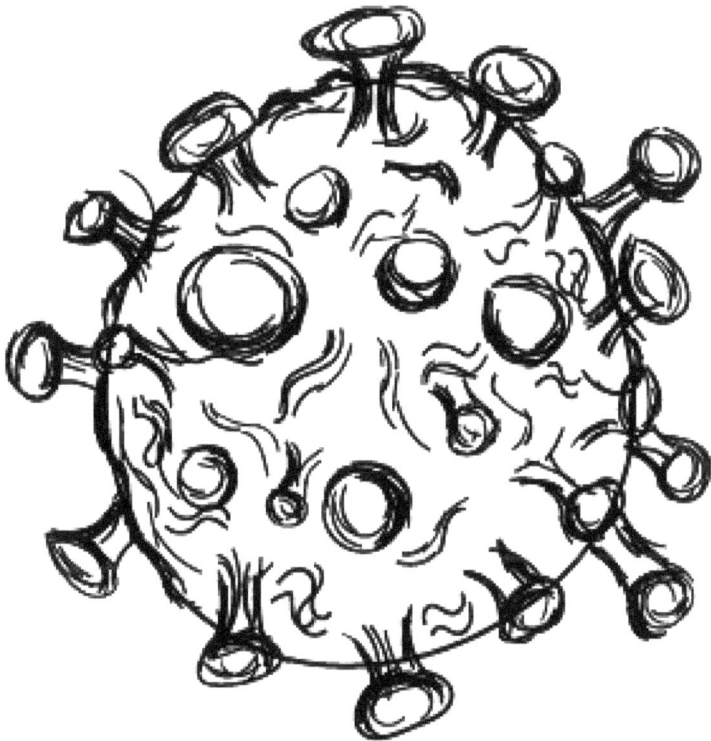

Stuck

She had the face of innocence

the body of a woman- but yet still a child

a young girl

Who didn't have much to worry about until she decided to take a step

into

woman-hood

her years too young to know what this part of life was all about

she had one foot in and the other was swaying back and forth on the

other side

STUCK

between two worlds

similar in some ways- but still very different

During this period in her life

a child was born

Still young- but now the face that she wears is old

and her body still intact but feeling very tired and worn out

And now that foot that was dangling on the other side

can't be brought back over

because now this young woman has to stand on her own two feet

Crush

❤️

Every time we see each other we have this........ I won't say bullshit
conversation
I'll keep it cute and say "small talk"
nothing too heavy at all, but right now I'm not sure if I fumbled or
completely dropped the ball (it's either that or your just not interested
at all) because right now I'm 0 for 3
and I'm just tryna see what you like
besides sneaks, weed, the pus and those bikes
It's the unspoken words with your eyes - it's this unwavering thing or
desire
fuck around with me, and I'll have you on a missing for 48 hours flyer
but you won't be missing for real
you'll just be somewhere exclusive…….. just enjoying the feel
of *things*

So next time I see you, can we get into the meat & potatoes
talks over drinks about sex and weather in Turks and Caicos
(You know) private conversations at a private location, let's have
breakfast baby, have lunch have dinner back to breakfast -maybe?

Hi Handsooooome, I'm Meek and I'm patiently waiting

for you to switch that red light to green, since the times we see each
other are too far and in between
but no pressure, no rush, just want you to know I've got this crush-- on
you--
^and I had a little too much to say to fit in a haiku^ besides.....................
grown folks don't play games they make moves

-I've got this crush on you –

☐ YES

☐ NO

☐ MAYBE

Are You Atleast Thinking About It?

No, Thank You

*

Him: Wait it's not all the way in
Her: What? … What you mean?

Umm Scuse me, what you think you doing with that?
you're not messing up MY walls
you see I need my walls to stay up, so this hole remains small
I think we're just going to have to be friends
because you will never get the chance to try and fuck me again
I would like to give ole girl who's taking that
some dap for that
Good luck with the next bitch
sorry but not sorry for my sudden exit
But
we not doing this
There will be no do overs
no retries
you see my frame is not built for dicks of that size
most I can do is pull up on you and talk to you outside
but we can't slide
Lesson learned, looks can be deceiving
but that's just too much dick that I'm willing to receive and
He called my girlfriend the next day with jokes
because it was smack dead in the middle of winter and I hauled ass
without my coat.

Life.... (Part 1)

What is this thing called life
why must I feel so stressed and depressed?
Is it me?
Where did I go wrong, because I'm tired of singing the same ole song
every time I think I'm on the right path, I start to lose my sight, my
grip
shiiit I think I'm losing my bop and my bip but I can't be out here
chasing dick
when half of these niggas ain't shit
It takes two to make a relationship, but I'm the only one willing to
commit
or am I really to young and need to live my life
Maybe I'm too young to be called somebody's wife
but every time I go out there, I don't see anything for me
So I thought that being home and having a family is where I need to be
because what I see
Is lies, lost souls, sex and scandals, real women that these weak men
can't handle
I see boys not men

I'm starting to believe the saying that all the good ones are either gay or
locked in the pen
caught in the system, is anybody really listening?
To the cries of our sons, our daughters they need attention
their souls need redemption

So is life really what you make it - or is it a bitch and then you die
cause there were so many nights and days I cried
Seems like I can't get ahead
went from being on my own to back at my mom's in that tight ass
room
on a twin size bed
I'm 21 plus, seems like I'm walking the path of the unknown
with 2 kids and responsibilities, I'm supposed to be grown
Am I really smart? or do I just pretend to be
and all this shit I go through is it really intended for me
Choices have consequence and consequence is no coincidence so

hence-the saying
It's a cold cold world, and I don't know my place in it
I'm just trying to figure out my purpose here, I'm just trying to see my
face in it
Shit I know good from bad, right from wrong
I know when a nigga ain't shit, and when he's doing me wrong
Do I really know what love is and although I can't sing
please allow me this moment to quote Vivian Green by singing
"What is looove, and if this isn't love – then tell me what is looove
maybe I will never know what's really looove, you got me feeling some
kind of way"
Searching for love in all the wrong places, tell me why do I keep
searching in all the wrong faces
Is my daughter going to be the same?
and who's to blame
Is it me for laying down at such an early age?
or her father for not being a good father....
Or my father for not wanting to be bothered with his Baby girl
left me all alone in this cold cold world.

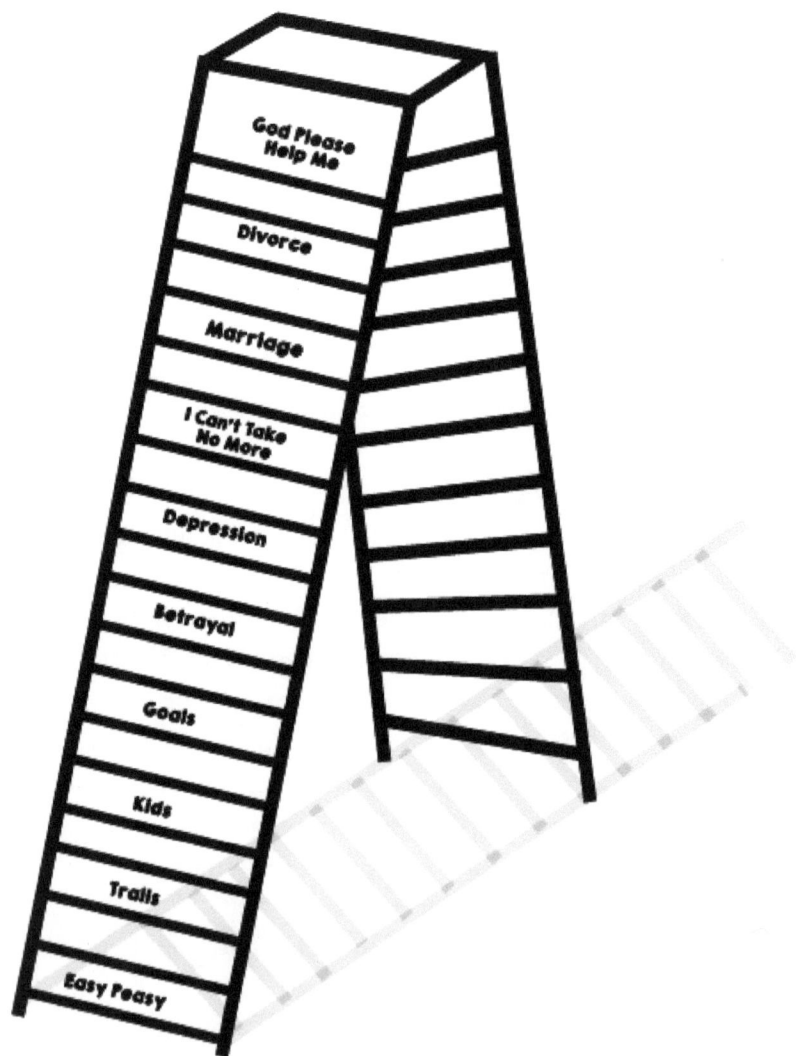

God Please
Help Me

Divorce

Marriage

I Can't Take
No More

Depression

Betrayal

Goals

Kids

Trails

Easy Peasy

Is It OK?

Is it ok for me to surrender -all the feelings I have inside of me
or should I just go on as the great pretender
acting as if all the things you do just don't bother me
Acting as if -------the way you touch me ----doesn't feel good to me
and like ya kisses don't taste like -a- fucking Sunday meal to me
Is it ok when we make love, to let the freak come out of me
to love you slowly and passionate
giving you everything I have inside of me?
I know there are some parts that I'm still holding on to
and I don't want those parts to jeopardize me losing you
So is it ok?
see I just have to be 212% sure
even though it's not your fault for the past pain that I've endured
So can I turn all my fears into this great big love affair?
is it ok for me to tell my other male friends, that in no way do they
compare
and that what I've found in you is real and rare
See it's kinda funny because I never thought that everything I wanted in
a man you'd be
and even though you put everything in my eye sight
it still seems as if I can't see
So why can't I just……… let it go
damn why can't I just…………………let shit flow
and even though everything is good, I'm still telling my friends "well I
just don't know"
Is it ok for me to get a lil deep and tell you a looove poem?

so instead of when you tell me how you feel, in return you get
silence and no words spoken
Is it ok for me to tell you how much I've missed you at the end of the
day
and tell you how I really feel despite my feelings that one day you'll go
astray
Is it really ok?
see you're so….. so….. sweet and passionate, sincere and affectionate
so why am I still second guessing it
The I miss you's…… I wanna see you's
I wanna give it all back
but I just can't seem to get this damn luggage off my back
So is it ok? ……………Hmm baby……..is it really ok?

Sure

Unsure

Dont want to let my guard down

THANK YOU
For Your Service
You Are My Hero

Fuck Buddy

*

It would be fly if you were my B-U-D-D-Y
only talk when it's time for a late night
no date nights
no texting
just sexting
we don't catch feelings here
we smash and leave it there
we talk when it's time to link
and we cool on the shallow conversations in between
when you have a "Fuck Buddy" we all know what that "wassup" means
when it comes across the phone screen
no strings
no attachments
just tricky positions and bending over backwards
fair exchange, no robbery
quid pro quo
just please don't forget to lock the door when you exit
but hypothetically speaking
if you stay would that go against the fuck buddy code of ethics?

Asking for a friend

The Ride to Daddy's Job

On the way to daddy's job, there is a long road that gets us there
there aren't a lot of travelers heading in the same direction
The road that is almost empty
has hills
some small, some large
on and behind them are large trunks
standing tall with tilted branches
While the sun-which had set
not too long before we started our journey
shines partially upon them
Most of them are naked, others have some clothing
and there are those that are fully clothed
There are houses
scattered here and there
There isn't much talk or conversation on this journey
instead we listen to lyrics, rhythms and harmonies
with anticipation of seeing our loved one
Wondering when he will be able to take this journey
this long road that separates us
this road that will bring him all the way home

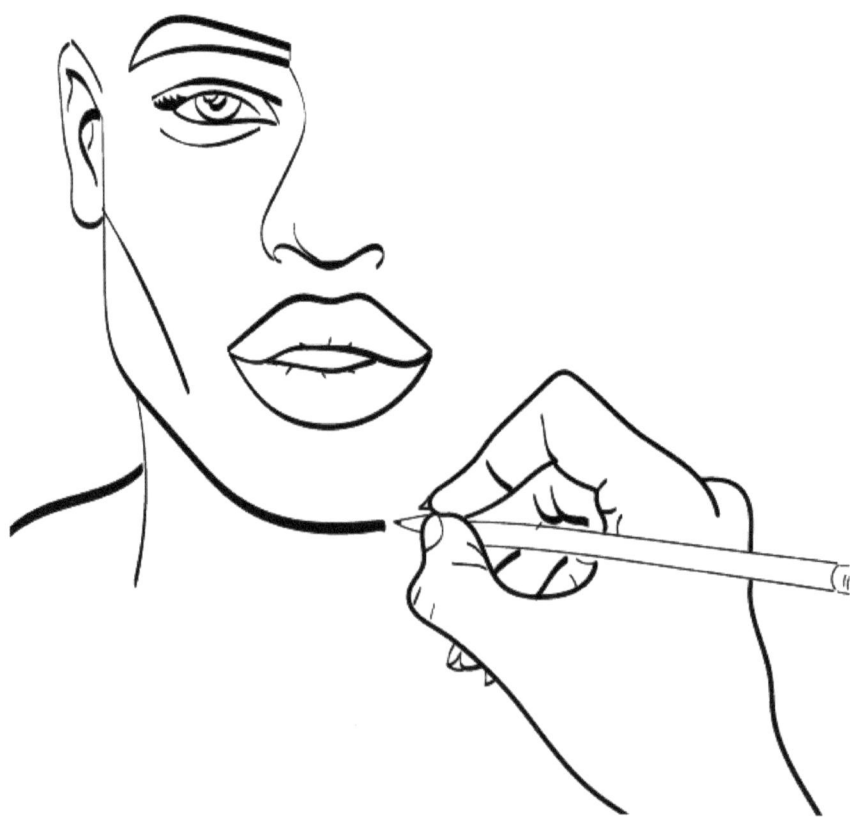

You

Thug, street smart with common sense and a gentleman
something about that combination
that raises my adrenaline
He's not lacking a thing, all that other shit is cool
but I'll take substance over everything
Because if anyone can have it, I don't want it
(I'm a sucker for realness and substance)
I like em untouchable, hard to get to, unfuckablewith
man it's something about a street nigga
that dances to the rhythm of his own beat nigga
I kiss you just to miss you
didn't think I could get so lucky
to have you fuck me, before you even touched me!

YOU

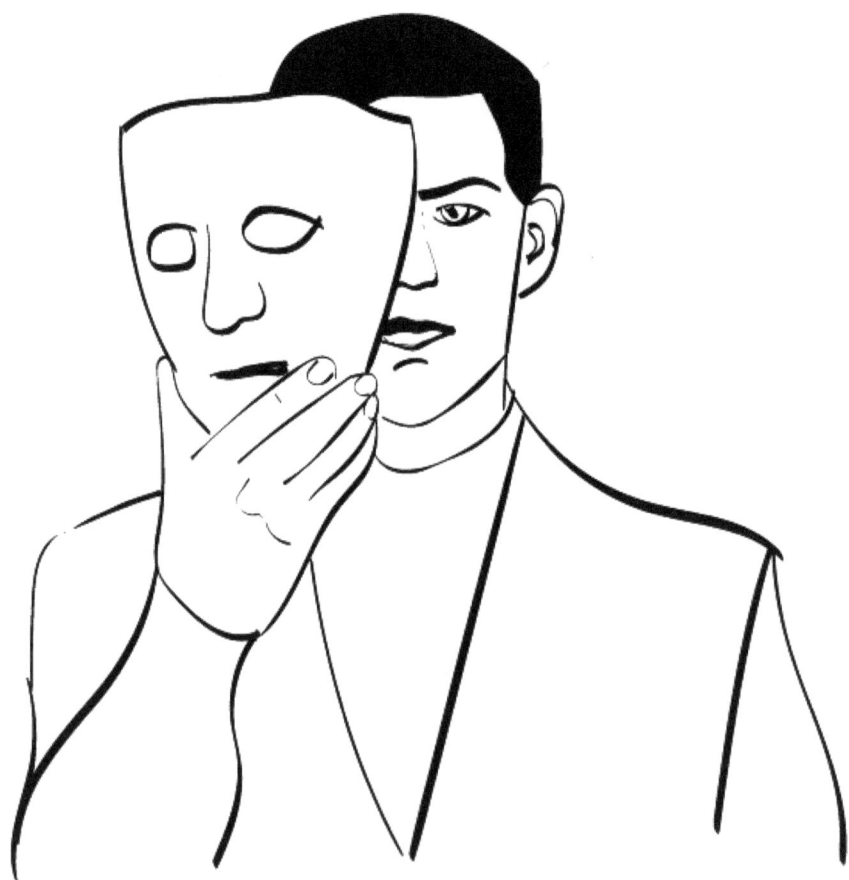

Mask Off

*

I need you to know how to handle me without me telling you how to handle me

I'm not interested in a perception of what you think I want to see

just keep this thing all the way real and not just as real as you want it to be

I need to see the real you

I like deep conversations, I need to know what makes you, you

and you will see a change or hear me complain

when the things done in the beginning you no longer make an effort to do

(I'm not mad at any of it)

Just be consistent on whatever side you choose

and I'll make sure I'll never confuse -what I'm offered for what I'm worth

So pick a side and stay there

and I'll decide if I wanna be here

no confusion

no smoke & mirrors and no illusions

Please go play with something safe
you don't want the smoke that's behind this resting bitch face

anything I require, I can reciprocate

I don't need you for anything

so please don't try to impress me with material things

It won't work

I'm on a soul search

No more trying to see the potential in what someone could be

less attention to their words and more of what their showing me

You can fake what you told me, but you can't fake what you showed me

and I can't make you into what I want you to be

I can't cut through anymore red tape, my scissors are dull

just be transparent

Bottom line is............

don't come to me trying to be someone else

because I will kindly tell you to take that shit somewhere else

I don't have time to play build a nigga …………..because I will kill you Niiiiiiiiga!!!

Mask off….. Please and thank you

P.S. All cards have to be on the table….. Besides I need a spades partner

Divorced not Desperate

If what you're showing me is the best that you can come up with
then let me remind you that
I'm divorced not desperate
How I move will depend on you
but I'll have to pump my brakes if doing the bare minimum becomes
an issue

because if the bare minimum is an issue
well then
we have an issue

My time is valuable and for most hard to get
so please don't forget
I have options
so if your actions don't match your words
I'll probably choose not to opt-in
I don't ask for much, that's why this shit is non-negotiable
and don't get caught up by the mean look on my face that reads I'm
unapproachable
I'm very easy to talk to
but again, how I move depends on you
So in case you haven't caught on yet
that means how I treat you
how I love you
how I fuck you

it's all on you

This isn't hard, it's like simple math $1 + 1 = 2$

no long division, or algorithms

no pies or square roots

just transparency and real truths

so if you're good at math, I promise you will eat the fruits

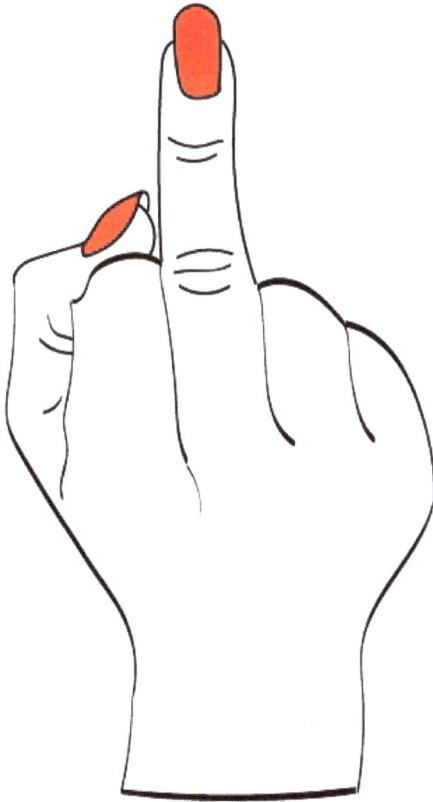

of your labor

Cover Me

You swallow me whole with no regurgitation
let me out this choke hold
I CAN'T BREATHE
Never thought I'd be gasping for air because of the way someone is
loving me
but I asked God to send someone to cover me
Friendship, kinship
love, passion
this is a *anything-ship*
homey, lover, friend
this is some *everything shit*
my bip to my bop
my ying to my yang
my boo thang
my twin flame
I hope you prayed for me
and now I hope that you pray for me
My soul has been suffering from 6 degrees of separation
My heart has been suffering from too many years of desperation
Strong but gentle
sexy, smart, funny, God-fearing
shit fucks with my mental
in a good way
I breathe you- I need you
if you could see inside my soul you'd see you

I need you to take the lead and teach me some things

because I asked God to send someone to cover me
So......... who sent you?
because if you wasn't sent by God
I'll have to respectfully decline
because (singing in my drake voice) you might just be here for a good
time not a long time
you know I
Don't wanna have to fuck you up sir!!

Situationship

*

See I know we not exclusive
but the truth is
I don't want anyone else to feel what I feel when you touch me
I don't want anyone else to feel what I feel when you love me

So call me selfish
you can probably even call me a little jealous

When it comes to how I feel about you
I try not to be over zealous
but I can't help it

That's my nigga
I'm his bitch
but we're not in a relationship

I'm Not Your Punching Bag

I'm not your punching bag

you can't raise a hand to me every time you get mad
You can't control me by hitting me every time you don't like something
that I said
I'm not your property
I know you want to limit where I go so you can watch over me
I can't speak my mind
I can't tell you how I feel
because if it goes against anything you say you will ……….
but I'm not your punching bag
If you could put me in a bubble you would
If you could keep me locked up and have me all to yourself
you'd keep me from the outside world

I'm not your punching bag

You can't raise a hand to me every time you don't like something that I
did

I only wanted you
but you couldn't handle anyone else wanting me but you
I'm too young for this mental and verbal abuse
what a price to pay for loving you

You want to control what I say
what I wear
where I go
And if I do anything that you don't like
Well……..
up your hand goes
It's not me
It's you
It's your own issues inside that causes you to question everything I do

I'm not your punching bag

You can't raise a hand to me every time you don't like something that I
said
You can't raise a hand to me every time you don't like something that I
did
or every time you get mad
I didn't even do anything all that bad

Why don't you go hit on one of these niggas when you get mad!

You Know You Turn Me On, Right?

❤️

You know you turn me on right?

And it has nothing to do with what takes place when you turn off
those lights
well maybe a little……….. shit
who I am fooling

I just picture us
laid up ---doing us---
not giving a fuck

Have I ever told you how much I love the sound of your voice?
It's the tone you use when you talk to me, then it's the tone you use
when you're inside of me
you know exactly what I like

You know you turn me on right?

I love the way you think and how you smell, how you can take one look
at me and tell
if something is bothering me
you are my muse

I love how you inspire me

You pay close attention
so I hope I never forget to mention
what you mean to me
or take you for granted
let's grow these seeds we planted

You know my flaws and you still accept me for me
because God knows I'm not perfect
scared to trust but easy to love
and I promise you I'm worth it

These niggas come a dime a dozen but he's the only one past &
present
that can calm me down with four words
I think he's connected to my soul

Seems you have me all figured out
but if I'm being honest let me tell you what really spooked me out

See I was told when praying to be specific
so as I was praying and going through the list of things I want in a man
I had to stop mid-sentence
and I asked GOD….. is this for real??
Is this you??
because we all know the devil comes in disguise because he can hear
our prayers too!

I said Lord if it's not of you please remove it, and if it's not from you
don't let this thing move forward
but guess what, he's still around
and only time will tell the rest

But for right now

If he's rocking --- I'm rolling
If he's strutting ---I'm strolling
He's my hitter --- I'm his killer

You know you turn me on right?

It's all mental for me
so it's not your ***exterior*** but your ***interior*** that gets me wet
and I still think its some things you haven't told me
still some things you haven't showed me
but I'm open
to receive it all

You know you turn me on right?

Naw seriously did you know?

As I Am (No Additives or Preservatives)

*

I have no armor left
you stripped me of it
whatever is left of me
It's yours
but please take note on what you signed up for
I come with past hurts & pains
jealousy moments
I'm far from perfect
and there can be some mood swings in between
but I'm still asking that you take all of me
It's a package deal and you can't just take part of me
I know it's not all good
I'm broken
but I promise to always show tokens of my appreciation
And in return you'll get loyalty, passion and reciprocation
and so much more
And I promise those things will outweigh the flaws
and the love that I give will outweigh them all
So again I'm asking that you take of all me
my feelings have been tucked away in a little box
for future use
I keep them in this safe place
so in the interim they won't be misused

TIRED OF HAVING MY GUARD UP – I've built this wall up
I guess were all a little broken
still waiting for this box to be opened
and some pieces still may not fit together

Are you good at puzzles?

Nutrition Facts

Serving size : 1

	% Daily Value
Moody	30%
Potty Mouth	30%
Broken	10%
Hard to Figure Out	30%
Solid	100%
Daily recommendation... good heart, loveable, ambitious focused	100%

* Percent Daily Value may vary

I Can't

You ever find yourself in a fucked up situation
and feeling like you've been the subject of constant manipulation

The how and whys did I end up here
even though signs were posted along the way
way before you ended up here

Sometimes it takes a while before people show their true colors
and it's just a matter of time before we discover the masked faces
among us

They say believe who people show you they are the first time

Energy takers
the older we get red flags are no longer warning signs
they become deal breakers

Morning After

Can we do this again?
the feeling of bare skin
touching the sheets

I think we should do this often & repeatedly

Can you smell that?
the scent of fresh warm air seeping through the windows

and you laying behind me

As we start to wake up, you slide your arm around me and pull me in
we lay there for a moment in silence
then we make love again

after a long night
I lay there and soak it all in

Can you feel that?

the energy is just ....
It's just high
and the night before
just felt right

Just me and you in the moment
no distractions
or outside disturbance
of any kind

His back is sun kissed
kisses as sweet as a drop of honey dew mist
and the dick is just ridiculous

I think it was made for *me*

That's why I said we need to do this often and repeatedly

Hate this part of the day
when we prepare to go our separate ways
Damn I hate to see you go
BUT FIRST COFFEE!!......... Cream & Sugar??

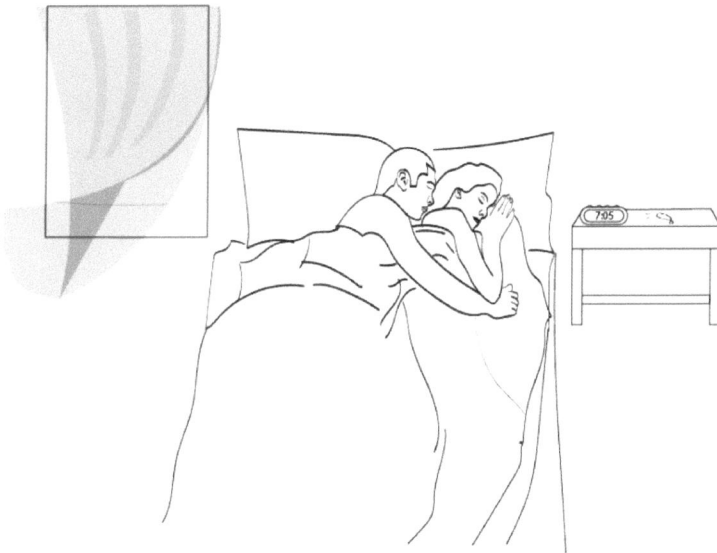

Us vs. Them

*

They say all men are created equal but when I look at the sentencing guidelines all I see is injustice when it comes to our people

They want the law to be respected - but how likely is that when you have laws in place that are based on misperception

The system is unethical & skeptical
they try to trick us by saying things like I want what's best for you

I'm sick of the racial imbalance
this shit is racially biased
tell me how a low level crack dealer gets more time then a wholesale supplier

So shout out to Barack Obama-
for passing the Fair Sentencing Act to even out the difference between the white folks selling powder and the black folks selling crack

He eliminated the minimum 5 year sentence and not to mention - they said crack was more addictive, but we all know crack was for blacks cause it was cheap and coke was more expensive
so damn right it was a difference
just not the way they made it appear to be - and if you pay close attention shit is just a different form of slavery.

Look at the rate they booking us, they cooking us, they roofing us

so let's not be completely oblivious
that this shit is happening to us
It's unfair and unjust

By the way, this is the law that got a lot of our people out of prison
and some after already serving 11 years of a 22 year sentence
Said he was coming to show up and show out and that's exactly what
he did
then he linked up with congress to try to right some wrongs for a
system that's rigged

BLACK
LIVES MATTER

Unusual Suspects

Moral of the story is this
these streets don't give a fuck about you and they don't owe you shit
After a while it gets hard trying to figure out who's who --- are they
frenemies or enemies
got you fucking playing Blue's Clues
OG said never underestimate a nigga or over trust him
fake friends and foes
your right hand man is the one that's been talking to them folks
They say the streets lead to one or two roads
death or Prison-stop trying to beat the system
you can't escape it
And if my numbers serve me correctly
the death toll average rate is…
Umm…. let's just say those numbers are high
and when you mix statics with ballistics
shit get kinda wiiicked
Smarten up, tighten up and keep your circle small
don't let greed be the reason for your downfall
It's called the laws of gravity
what goes up, must come down
And all those niggas you was running wit and all those bitches you was
fucking wit
ain't gone be nowhere to be found
C'mon yall, we all know how the story ends
Same story…. Different Hood
and just a different group of friends

We all got that one in our crew
and for the power – that yolk – that ego stroke – that juice....
He's coming for you and you and you and you!

Holding On

At one time in our lives, we felt as if our love was unbreakable
and to hold onto to it forever, we felt as if we were
cable
but times changed, and our situation became rearranged
The love that we once felt before, was no longer the love that we both
endured
I've been waiting for so long – for you to sweep me back off my feet
you were my first love so tender, so sweet
Everything seemed so right back then, but when you would come back
into life
I didn't know when
but for some reason we were both still holding on
not knowing what to do to make things right
HUH-WE WAS A MOTHER FUCKER together
our thing use to be tight
Still don't know what the future holds, will it make room for a love that
is old
all these years of trying to make things right, what was it all for?
They say when it rains it pours
because now it seems like we're far apart than ever before.

S.E.X.

*

The room is dark, but slightly lit
from surrounding candles
The mood is right
and we're listening to the sounds of Marvin Gaye
mixed with a little bit of Barry White
I start to feel this wetness on my lips
then to my neck
between my breast
all the way down to my belly button
of lips so soft and sensuous
I feel hands caressing my entire body softly
making me feel completely at ease
As I lay there
I quickly recall everything that has happened
and how this situation came to be
and I prepare myself as I indulge this warm
sensation inside of me

Life (Part II)

Why weren't you around dad?
there were so many special moments that we could have had
so many things that were important to me
so many things that I wanted you to see
like what a beautiful young woman I turned out to be……

Funeral day, I thought I wouldn't cry
but then the tears came falling from all the wishing things were
different and all the pain I felt inside
How could you just go on every day, just leaving us in the wing?
as if we didn't exist or we didn't mean a thing -to you-
You couldn't have thought not being around was the right thing to do
I guess the streets had you by the balls
and you don't even know it
but you were the cause ……….of so many things
like me
looking for love in all the wrong faces
like me
looking for love in all the wrong places
And all I ever wanted to be - was Daddy's Little Girl
but you left me all alone in this cold cold world
So is life really what you make it?
or is it a Bitch and then you die…..
Cause there were sooo many nights and days I cried

Victory

One More Step

Peace

Prayer Faith Belief

Pain

Let Me Love You

Let me love you - all I wanna do is love you
not sure, how much more I have to do to get through to you
and prove to you
that - all I wanna do is love you

Seems like everyone is worried about who's gonna play who
and in this day and age everyone is too cool

Can we take these walls down and just live in the moment
remove any past wounds and become current
with each other

I don't want to get hurt and you don't want to get hurt either
but let's not hold things up because whatever is gone be is gone be and
if we both holding back from the fear of getting hurt
tell me how the fuck this suppose to work

You see time is of the essence -shit the way I see it ain't no better time
than the presence
so let's take a step in the right direction

Imperfectly a perfect fit, come over here and let me love on you a lil bit

(You're just a habit I don't wanna kick)

So what's up?....Are you down for long walks
long talks
silly and serious moments
while we try to understand each other and put together these
components

I promise to be there when you need me
I'm willing to take the necessary steps
and I promise to love you at both your worse and your best

You trump everything

Baby all I want is you

Let me love you -all I wanna do is love you

You ready or Naw?

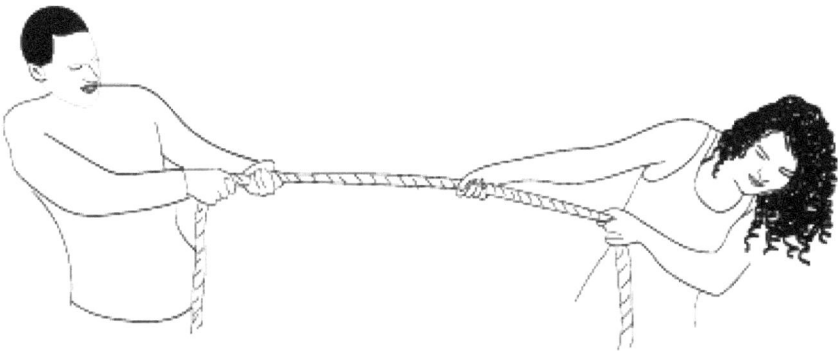

Her

*

I'm too old to be telling someone how to fuck with me
and I'm too grown to be jumping from nigga to nigga,
so stop asking my girlfriend what's up with me
I'm not interested
You gotta come already assembled if you wanna fuck with me
my real and your real don't match
the body---------- snatched

I promise you can check around, but I'm checking all boxes
even though I suffer from a broken heart and disappointments way too
often
So trusting
So giving
even in this fucked up world we live in

The thoroughness has nothing to do with looks

she's street smart, good folks and she fucks with them books
She ages gracefully
and I'm looking for a nigga that can kneel down and pray with me
pray for me
come fuck with me
come lay with me
be bae for me
come stay with me
and tell them bitches don't come for me

☑ SEXY

☑ SMART

☑ HOOD

☑ CLASSY

☑ WITH THE SHITS

We Not the Same, Sis

*

Bitches wondering what's the hype
these niggas wondering what it's like
 is the pussy good?
what type of niggas she like? …And yea I can be freaky but that all
depends on who you asking
how turned on I am, who's the nigga and how strong is the attraction

I got a lot of love inside of me and I've put a lot of hurt behind me
they say I'm mysterious, hard to gauge, they have no idea who I really
am
but I think that's when the turn on comes in

But what you see is what you get
99 percent of the time humble but just a friendly reminder that
I'm the shit
and I don't want to be in anyone else's shoes because I got my own and
I like the way they fit

I'm sorry damn, I forgot to mention that my tongue a lil slick

Built from the inside out not the outside in, and I like to talk shit every
now and again
I stay in my own lane which means I never tried to fit in
I get to be myself, be free, be me, so to me that's a win win

I've seen niggas that could never reach me
come after my seed
cause she's a -rep-li-ca of meeee....
you see the irony

I'm either all the way in or all the way out
no gray areas
tricks are for kids
and this here is
no play area
Everything I've got I've earned and everything I'm about to get I
deserve

Risk taker, goal chaser, shit talking heart breaker with a big heart
who's sexy whether in sweats or a dress
so check my style and while you at it -peep my walk
it's mean

And I don't get chosen, I do the choosing- so it's zero fucks given
about how someone else is moving
I Come from good stock (singing) Nigga ask about me nigga ask about
me……..

So FYI if you're coming for me, I'm looking for something
extraordinary
because I'm pretty much done with the mediocre, the just ok and the
ordinary ....shit

All experiences moving forward, need to be mind blowing
from the sex, to the conversation, to the gifts, to the trips

You know since I got my heart patched, I wanna be able to call my
sister and be like Biiiiiiitch

I think I got my soul snatched!!!!! ..... Any takers??

So you see -my *DIFFERENCE* has always made me *DIFFERENT*
and yea I'm a lot of things rolled up in one
and yes it's plenty bitches with the same characteristics but
I'm still *ONE* of *ONE*

We not the same sis

BE YOU DIFFERENT WE ARE NOT THE SAME ONLY ONE OF ME

I Like You (Part 2)

Told you- you won me over with your smile
but did I tell you that your smile makes me smile
so many layers, looks and thoughts at a first glance can be deceiving
which is just a turn on
and makes it more pleasurable when I'm receiving…. You
This one of a kind you
love when you grab on me and kiss me from behind
feels like our souls intertwine… our bodies are aligned
(Like a seat belt something connected) something just clicked
and I'm trying my best through my poems to explain this shit
because when it comes to these words I considered myself to be pretty
articulate
But shit
Feels like I'm in the matrix, replaying things in my head
like a certain way you looked at me, or a certain thing that you said
Or maybe it's my own mind playing tricks on me, because we all know
how the mind works
when these things are said when they get in our beds
Got me feeling like …………………what's that song?
(Singing) "I really like when you fuck on me" or whatever Tamia said
I'm too old for this for Pete's sake
I just wanna take a moment from a moment and hold it for a mental
keepsake
So! If this is all a ruse… just put the blind fold on me now
because this feature is no longer starring Sandra Bullock but its starring
TAMIKA NICOLE now!

(He made it to part 2 yall)

My Journey

I am a black woman, proud mother, good lover and friend,
November 18, 1976 is when my journey began, I don't know when my
journey will end
but until then
My test will continue to be my testimonies
not all good but still grateful for the favor and blessings HE bestowed
upon me
I am passionate, unapologetic, bold & fierce
and when I'm gone, I know I'll leave my mark behind
So you will know I was here

Tamika Nicole

A Note from the Author

I really hope you enjoyed the book but before I go I would just like to give you a few words of encouragement and leave you with a few things to remember besides my foolishness in these poems. ;)

I know sometimes in life when we have goals and aspirations they may seem hard to reach, and they can be but remember the day you plant the seed is not the day you eat the fruit. When you plant a seed you have to water it in order for it to grow right? Same rules apply when it comes to your goals but you have to water them with ACTION in order to see them manifest.

It all boils down to how bad do you want it. You HAVE to put the work in, you can't skip that part. Faith without work is dead, and that takes dedication, consistency and mental toughness and you have to put GOD in it. It all starts with your mindset and your thought process.

Replace your Fear with Faith, I've learned a lot through failure. Make this shit count, be you, be happy, live the life you want. I tell my children we don't get any do-overs, we only have ONE life to LIVE. You are worthy of good things, keep pushing. CREATE YOUR OWN REALITY! .... Remember if you don't try you'll fail by default.

-Tamika Nicole

On the next page I want you to list your goals and break them down into steps. God made you unique don't ruin that trying to be like anyone else!

P.S. YOU GOT THIS!!

I want you to make a list of your goals here, put the work in and do the research, then make your plan of action below……. step by step that will get you to where you want to be whatever that may be.

GOAL 1   GOAL 2   GOAL 3

1.   1.   1.

2.   2.   2.

3.   3.   3.

4.   4.   4.

5.   5.   5.

NOW CRUSH THAT SHIT!!

DAILY AFFIRMATIONS

I CAN AND I WILL

I AM AMAZING

I AM FEARLESS

I AM ENOUGH

I AM WORTHY

I AM POWERFUL

I AM LIMITLESS

I AM THE SHIT!!!

About the Author

Tamika Nicole started writing poetry over 20 years ago. She took a liking to poetry in middle school and was intrigued with poets like Edgar Allan Poe. She starting writing then and has never stopped. As an adult, she began writing poems for obituaries, weddings and used her poetry as both a form of expression and an outlet. Tamika starting doing Open Mic events all over the City of Philadelphia. She was then spotted at the Laugh House by a local promoter who asked her to open at his comedy show. That led to her sharing the stage at various venues with multiple comedians including Philly's own Buckwild, Tu Rae, Spank Horton & more.

Tamika's writing style is focused on portraying real-life experiences. She takes pride in narrating stories that give voice to her unique perspective. To date, her pieces have been featured on poetry CDs, fashion documentaries and movie soundtracks. In the future, she hopes to explore screen play writing.

In addition to poetry, Tamika also writes children's literature. She is a youth advocate and was awarded a Citation of Honor & Recognition by the City of Philadelphia for her work in the community. Her personal passions include acting, fashion and she has a love for music and the outdoors. Tamika is a mother of two and currently makes her home in Haddon Township, NJ.

STAY TUNED...
for **VOLUME II** ....
I got some more shit to say!